An opinionated guide to

NEW
YORK

T0282143

DEVRA FERST

Agi's Counter (no.10)

INFORMATION IS DEAD.
LONG LIVE OPINION.

All guide books are useless. After all, everything you could possibly want to find out is available online for free. Right?

Wrong! Why go online into the netmare digital death-jungle to forage for information? What you want is simple, pared-back opinion. This is precisely what we offer you in this book (and check out the rest of our series online... yes, I realise I just told you not to go there). These are the places we'd send you if you decided to hang out with us, share a coffee and ask, 'Hey, you make nice books, where would should I REALLY go in NYC?'

New York is impossibly layered. Life is endlessly complex. It's all too much! Keep it simple and read our guide. Go!

Martin
Hoxton Mini Press

Above: Riegelmann Boardwalk (no.41)

BEAM (no.55)

Above: Wythe Hotel (no.91)
Right: The Hoxton, Williamsburg (no.90)

Central Park (no. 35)

FINDING YOUR NEW YORK

New York's defining feature is that there is no single New York; within the city are infinite coexisting New Yorks. The city is Joni Mitchell's 'Chelsea Morning' and Alicia Keys' pocketful of dreams. It's also bustling Queens with neighbourhoods like Jackson Heights with its thriving Thai, Nepalese, Indian and Colombian communities that help make the borough one of the most diverse urban areas on Earth. It's ballet fans *jeté*-ing to Lincoln Center (no.85) and joyful queer gatherings at West Village spot Cubbyhole (no. 78). It's delivery drivers on e-bikes zooming down streets at lightning speeds and chefs waking up at the crack of dawn to procure flawless produce from the Union Square Greenmarket (no.45).

This is a place where life is lived out loud. Infamously cramped apartments push New Yorkers out onto the streets and into beloved third places that become extensions of their homes. No matter who you are, New York is a place to truly be yourself – even at maximum volume – and find people who share your passions.

Whether you're a life-long New Yorker or visiting for the first time, the best way to do New York is on foot. The perfect day often doesn't involve a destination, just a starting point and a direction for exploration. Pick a neighbourhood like the East Village, home to micro-shops dedicated to everything from rubber stamps to eclectic homewares (no.49), or quirky Red Hook, with its dive bars and waterfront views. Or opt for a storied street like Broadway, which runs the length of Manhattan, past the wrought-iron buildings of SoHo up to Union Square, through the glaring lights of Times Square, onto Lincoln Center and then all the way up to The Bronx. Stop for a slice of pizza – you're never far from pizza here – and a jolt of coffee to keep you going, or a nightcap if it's after dark. Lost? Yes, New Yorkers are notoriously brusque, but ask for directions and you might be surprised by how many will offer guidance, especially when it comes to navigating the crumbling subway – something every New Yorker has a love-hate relationship with.

It's almost impossible to write a single guide to the infinite New Yorks that exist. But this is ours: it's filled with awe-inspiring art, legendary bookshops, iconic urban parks and standout restaurants. While exploring, always remember to look around – pop into that shop you glimpsed down the street, the gallery with a packed opening you just walked past, the tiny community garden with its gate invitingly open. Eight and a half million people call this city home, and each has their own New York. Getting to know the city means finding yours – and we're happy to help.

Devra Ferst
New York, 2024

Devra Ferst is a food and travel writer who has called New York City home for over 20 years. Her work has appeared in the New York Times, Vogue, Bon Appetit *and* Eater. *She is also the co-author of* The Jewish Holiday Table: A World of Recipes, Traditions & Stories to Celebrate All Year Long. *You can often find her racing around New York on her green bicycle, Olive.*

BEST FOR...

Cultural Offerings

New York's cultural calendar can feel frenetic, but kicking things off at the Met (no.66), the queen of museums, is always a good idea. Head to Lincoln Center (no.85) if you prefer your art onstage. Downtown, the Judd Foundation (no.70) and David Zwirner (no.75) provide creative energy.

Iconic New York fare

Competition for the greatest burger, pizza and bagel is fierce. Visit Red Hook Tavern (no.18) for the Platonic ideal of the burger, Scarr's (no.17) for a superior slice made with house-milled flour and PopUp (no.25) for fresh bagels.

Natural escapes

Green escapes are vital for survival in this concrete jungle. Central Park (no.35) and Prospect Park (no.36) are both tranquil and spacious enough to offer a mental reset, or go further afield and enjoy the sea breeze on the Riegelmann Boardwalk (no.41). In spring, visit the cherry blossoms at the Brooklyn Botanic Garden (no.37).

Old New York

Follow up a visit to the Tenement Museum (no.67) with dinner in the Gilded Age-style dining room at Gage & Tollner (no.20). Break your fast with gleaming slices of lox at Russ & Daughters (no.7), which has been 'appetizing since 1914'.

Shopping

Casa Magazines (no.62) and the Strand's (no.63) '18 miles of books' are mandatory stops for readers. If it's homeware you're after, do a double hit at John Derian (no.53) for his signature decoupage pieces, then Coming Soon (no.49) for more technicolour delights.

Pastries

Seasonal rhubarb and custard croissants at Radio Bakery (no.24) are worth the wait, and you should make it your mission to visit Lysée (no.27) for delicate madeleines. Miraculously, the crunchy, ricotta-filled sfogliatelle (shell-shaped pastry) at Un Posto Italiano (no.23) still fly under the radar.

Rainy Days

Pair a visit to the marble splendour of Bergdorf Goodman (no.54) with a tuna melt or a pastrami Reuben at S&P Lunch (no.15). Alternatively, stick to the Lower East Side with a film at Metrograph (no.86) and exceptional Neapolitan pizza at Una Pizza Napoletana (no.33).

New York after dark

Catch a midnight jam session at Smalls (no.87), or a nightcap uptown at sleek Sugar Monk (no.80). If you're in the Village, queer bar Cubbyhole's (no.78) jukebox plays until 4am on weekends. Rather not cross the East River? The Long Island Bar (no.82) pours some of the best cocktails in the city.

A PERFECT WEEKEND

FRIDAY NIGHT

Toast Friday with a jazz set at Smalls (no.87) in the West Village, then mosey over to queer destination Cubbyhole (no.78). To kick off the weekend in low-key Brooklyn fashion, take a dusky riverside stroll through Brooklyn Bridge Park (no.38) and sip a classic cocktail at The Long Island Bar (no.82).

A Saturday in Manhattan

SATURDAY MORNING

There's no greater joy than a sunny Saturday wandering the Union Square Greenmarket (no.45). Weave through the maze of vendors then make a beeline for a hearty diner breakfast at S&P Lunch (no.15) or Abraço (no.8) for an espresso con panna (with cream).

SATURDAY MIDDAY

See old New York at the Tenement Museum (no.67), snag a slice at Scarr's Pizza (no.17) then browse the colourful homeware at Coming Soon (no.49). Alternatively, catch a subway uptown to the Met (no.66) then duck into Central Park (no.35) for a breather afterwards.

SATURDAY EVENING

Aim for a reservation at dynamic South Indian spot Semma (no.13) or Cervo's (no.11) for Iberian coastal fare. If you're looking for entertainment, scan the listings at The Public (no.77) – or Lincoln Center (no.85) if you're itching to don your opera gloves.

A Sunday in Brooklyn

SUNDAY MORNING

Wake up with a cappuccino at Un Posto Italiano (no.23); make friends with a regular to snag a section of their newspaper. Had a late night? Tuck into Hungarian crepes at Agi's Counter (no.10). If you're near Bushwick, head to SEY Coffee (no.26) for grade-A people-watching.

SUNDAY MIDDAY

Work your way through North Brooklyn's shopping scene: visit BEAM (no.55) for Scandi homewares and McNally Jackson (no.46) for a new read. 50 Norman (no.52) serves an unbeatable Japanese lunch, or you could brave the line at Radio Bakery (no.24) for an extra-large sandwich. With your appetite sated, swing by Big Night (no.59) for fancy pantry goods.

SUNDAY EVENING

If sunset is approaching, head south to Valentino Pier (no.34) then eat a perfect burger at Red Hook Tavern (no.18). Alternatively, settle in for a pasta-filled evening at Roman's (no.1) to restore you for the week ahead.

N

2

MTA 79 St

W 72ND ST

MTA 72 St

35

CENTRAL PARK

E 65TH

HUDSON RIVER

BROADWAY

Grand Central 42 St
MTA

E 57TH

E 42ND ST

11TH AVE
10TH AVE
9TH AVE
8TH AVE
7TH AVE
6TH AVE
5TH AVE
PARK AVE
3RD AVE
2ND AVE
1ST AVE

34 St-Hudson Yards
MTA

E 34TH ST

Market 57
Little Island

68

E 23RD ST

EAST RIVER

MTA Houston St

E 14TH ST

Chambers St
MTA

CYCLE 1

Contemporary art, lunch with a view
and NYC icons up the Hudson

With a bike – or a Citi Bike day pass – put on your helmet and start pedalling north at Chambers Street, stopping off for some contemporary art at The Whitney **68** then meander over to *Little Island**, perched above the river on extraterrestrial-looking tulip-shaped pillars. Refuel with a rooftop lunch next door at *Market 57**, a food hall curated in collaboration with the James Beard Foundation. Get back in the saddle and keep moving uptown, past the gargantuan aircraft carrier the Intrepid at 46th Street, before catching your breath on Pier I, jutting out into the Hudson at 70th street. Continue on foot through Riverside Park over to the legendary gourmet market Zabar's **2** for picnic provisions, bringing your loot over to enjoy at Strawberry Fields in Central Park **35**.

Travel time: 1.5 hours, 7.9 miles
Total time with stops: 5 hours
*Not in guidebook: more info online

WALK 1

A meander through the West Side's charms

Set off from the top of the High Line **40** at 34th Street, working your way down the stunningly repurposed, elevated railroad tracks to enjoy the art installations and uniquely New York views. Hop off at the southern exit by The Whitney **68** and duck into the picturesque West Village. Weave your way up and down tree-lined streets, multimillion-dollar homes and groups of brunchers perennially packed into alfresco tables. Find your way to Casa Magazines **62** for a glossy you never knew existed, swing by Big Night **59** for gourmet dinner party provisions and a farfalle-shaped candle, then stroll to *Grove Court** for a glimpse of the 19th-century buildings and their quaint shared courtyard. Treat yourself to a Taiwanese tea tasting at Té Company **19** or gelato at Pamina **30**.

Walking time: 1 hour, 2.8 miles
Total time with stops: 2–3 hours
**Not in guidebook: more info online*

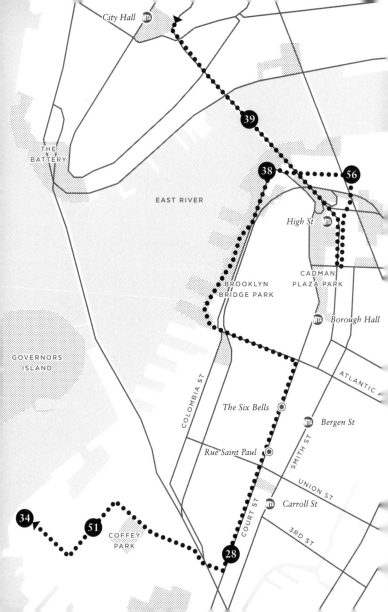

WALK 2

The big Brooklyn jaunt

Strap on some comfortable walking shoes and set out from the Manhattan side of the Brooklyn Bridge **39**, turning back every so often to take in the gobsmacking views. Once you've reached the Brooklyn side, work your way down to Dumbo for vintage scouting at Front General Store **56** before walking through Brooklyn Bridge Park **38**. See if you can catch a game of hoops on Pier 2 or rest your feet in the park on Pier 6. Hike up Atlantic Avenue or hop onto a Citi Bike to charming Court Street, popping into *The Six Bells** for country-chic home-ware and *Rue Saint Paul** for sustainable fashion. Refuel at Court Street Grocers **28** with a sandwich. Once restored, make your way to Van Brunt Street in the heart of quirky Red Hook to browse the stock at Open Invite **51** and then over to Valentino Pier **34** to take in the glorious view of The Statue of Liberty.

Walking time: 2.5 hours, 6.1 miles
Total time with stops: 5 hours
**Not in guidebook: more info online*

WALK 3

Straight down Broadway

Stretching from tip to tip of Manhattan, no street is more classically New York than Broadway; walk any segment and the city will transform before your eyes, one neighbourhood morphing into another. Start on the Upper West Side and stock up on snacks like rugelach (crescent-shaped pastries) at iconic food emporium Zabar's **2**, then head south, pausing at the Lincoln Center **85** fountain before girding your loins to traverse Times Square. Walk towards the Flatiron Building to restore yourself at S&P Lunch **15** with a straight-forward sandwich and a classic egg cream, made of seltzer, milk and chocolate syrup. Eye up luxe goods at abc carpet & home **61** and then mosey through Union Square – if it's Monday, Wednesday, Friday or Saturday, check out the greenmarket **45**. Pick out your next great read at the Strand **63**, straying from Broadway to go and enjoy it in Washington Square Park **42**.

Walking time: 1.5 hours, 4.4 miles
Total time with stops: 4–5 hours
*Not in guidebook: more info online

WALK 4

Village to Village to Village

New York really out New Yorks itself in the East Village, with wonderfully unique shops and restaurants that go all in. Start with lunch at Superiority Burger **14** or warm up with a bowl of udon noodles at Raku **21**. Stroll over to John Derian's **53** trio of stores on 2nd Street to trip out on the colourful aesthetic, or hang with photography obsessives below street level at Dashwood Books **58** on Bond Street, before heading to Greenwich Village. You may not run into Bob Dylan, but keep an eye out for more contemporary celebrities. Rest your feet in Washington Square Park **42** – you never know what you might find here. Protestors? Performers? A cannabis-themed festival? Finally, weave your way through the ultra-charming West Village for an intimate jazz set at Smalls **87**.

Walking time: 1 hour, 1.6 miles
Total time with stops: 4 hours
*Not in guidebook: more info online

1
ROMAN'S

The quintessential neighbourhood gem

More than a decade on, Andrew Tarlow's Fort Greene restaurant Roman's remains a stalwart favourite of neighbours, food writers and New Yorkers looking for a place that won't feel cramped or rushed. The menu is short but mighty, and changes daily according to the season. In winter, you might discover an artful salad with pink chicory; in springtime, strands of spaghetti gleam with melted onions, anchovy and dandelion greens. Come summer, sweet heirloom tomatoes make their mark on panzanella. Reservations are strongly recommended.

243 Dekalb Ave, Brooklyn, NY 11205
Nearest station: Clinton–Washington (G)
romansnyc.com

ROMAN'S

2

ZABAR'S

The connoisseur's grocery store

First opening its doors in 1934, Zabar's is a New York institution and an excellent reason to visit the Upper West Side. Unlike the omnipresent Whole Foods, Zabar's isn't trying to sell you a lifestyle – though its selection is still vast and highly desirable. What's different here is that they go deep into specialist varieties, evidenced in the famously lengthy and pungent cheese counter that greets visitors at the door, overflowing with teetering heaps of brie and precariously hanging smoked gouda, or their legendary smoked fish section that shifts 4,000 pounds weekly. If you're aiming for a picnic in Riverside or Central Park (no.35) there's no better place to stock up.

2245 Broadway, New York, NY 10024
Nearest station: 79th Street (1)
zabars.com

3

THAI DINER

Maximalist spot for inventive cooking

Wife-and-husband duo Ann Redding and Matt Danzer have been leaders in New York's Thai food scene for many years. Opening Thai Diner on the cusp of the pandemic, they miraculously made it through to the other side, and fans continue lining up for meals at the playfully kitsch, rattan-lined space, pairing muay Thai punch bowls for the table with Thai disco fries with massaman curry. Thai Diner's take on laab is a fiery salad that can be topped with crunchy fried chicken, and house specialities like the crab-loaded fried rice and snapper raad prik (crispy whole fish) that arrive at the table sizzling hot. End the meal with a whimsical dessert like the coffee monster cake – complete with edible eyes.

186 Mott Street, New York, NY 10012
Nearest station: Spring Street (6)
thaidiner.com

4

WU'S WONTON KING

Large tables for an even larger menu

Wu's is the type of Chinese restaurant that feels like its lazy Susans have been spinning since the dawn of time, though mysteriously the establishment hasn't yet reached its tenth birthday. At Wu's they aren't trying to do anything new; they are here to perfect the classics. Guests are greeted by burnished ducks hanging in the window, ready to be carved and tucked into perfectly puffy steamed buns. Waiters march a never-ending parade from kitchen to table, transporting fragrant wonton soup with plump shrimp dumplings and salty, golden chicken topped with crispy garlic. The dining room is always packed and eating here is best enjoyed with a crowd – reservations are only available for tables of six or more and if you walk in without one, expect a wait.

165 East Broadway, New York, NY 10002
Nearest station: East Broadway
wuswontonking.com

5

GRAND CENTRAL OYSTER BAR

Oysters and martinis in the world's biggest station

Since 1913, Grand Central Oyster Bar has shucked and served oysters under terracotta-tiled archways in the bowels of Grand Central Terminal, which dodged demolition before being declared a national landmark in 1975. Despite its age, they haven't lost their bearings; it's still a busy restaurant treasured by longtime New Yorkers. The menu is vast, with oysters from both the East and West Coasts – Blue Point oysters from Connecticut give you bang for your buck, while Cape May Salts from New Jersey are a terrifically briny palette cleanser. Grab a spot at one of the fast-moving counters if you have a train or show to catch; raw oysters and a dirty martini at the bar remains a bulletproof choice.

89 E 42nd Street, New York, NY 10017
Nearest station: Grand Central Terminal
oysterbarny.com

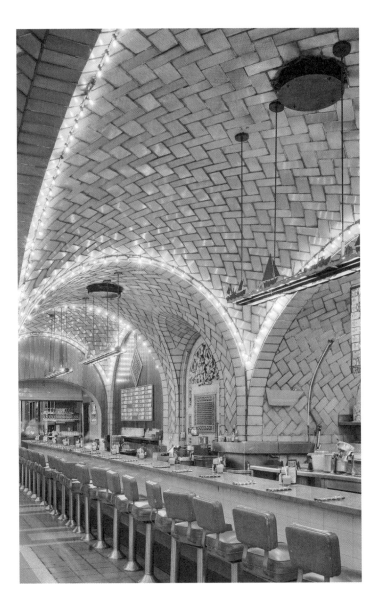

6

ESSEX MARKET

Abundant gastronomic variety

While Chelsea Market is packed with tourists, Essex Market is for locals, and has been for nearly a century. Opened in 1940 by Mayor Fiorello H. La Guardia (yes, as in LaGuardia airport), it moved into its current home in 2019 and now resides on the ground floor of the glossy Essex Crossing development – but there's still real soul here. Stop by Nordic Preserves Fish and Wildlife Company for slices of smoked or cured salmon and Formaggio Essex for cheeses from knowledgeable mongers. Seats for dinner at Indian restaurant Dhamaka at the northern edge of the market are rightly coveted – it's owned by the same unapologetically brilliant team behind Semma (no.13).

88 Essex Street, New York, NY 10002
Nearest station: Delancey Street–Essex Street
essexmarket.nyc

7

RUSS & DAUGHTERS

Herring, lox and other delights

Unless you grew up in a New York Jewish family, you might not be familiar with the concept of an *appetizing store*. While delicatessens like Katz's are pastrami palaces, shops like Russ & Daughters keep the focus squarely on bagels – and anything you might enjoy topping them off with; primarily, copious quantities of smoked and cured fish. Russ & Daughters has been a fixture of the Lower East Side since 1914, and the accolades keep rolling in. Go to East Houston Street for the complete experience, which will include being sandwiched between regulars who have been shopping there for decades, and who are quick to remind you to grab a ticket on your way in and wait your turn.

179 East Houston Street, New York, NY 10002
Nearest station: 2nd Avenue
Other locations: Brooklyn's Navy Yard, Hudson Yards
russanddaughters.com

8
ABRAÇO

Espresso, taken seriously

As coffee chains like Blank Street and Blue Bottle proliferate in New York, independent cafes have become increasingly scarce. Abraço in the East Village is a fiercely beloved exception that takes its name from the Brazilian song 'Aquele Abraço' ('that hug'). Once the size of a postage stamp, the shop moved to a much larger space across the street in 2016, but beware as it can still feel cramped on the weekends. Known for their uncompromising approach to espresso, this is the place to savour a double shot, classic cappuccino or espresso con panna (with cream). Wait for your order at the far end of the bar. Can't find a seat? Take your coffee to Tompkins Square Park a block away.

81 East 7th Street, New York, NY 10003
Nearest station: Astor Place
abraconyc.com

9

THE FOUR HORSEMEN

Wine-forward feasting

Arrive at The Four Horsemen in Williamsburg around 5:20pm and it's a safe bet you'll join an already sizeable line. Co-owned by LCD Soundsystem's James Murphy, wine industry insiders flock to this small natural wine bar and restaurant for sommelier Justin Chearno's marathon bottle list. For the more casual drinker, deeply knowledgeable yet highly unpretentious staff are on-hand to guide you towards the vino of your dreams. To accompany your choice, chef Nick Curtola's dishes pledge their allegiance to deliciousness rather than any particular cuisine, and you're just as likely to find spinach tonnarelli (spaghetti-like pasta) as you are veal sweetbread skewers with soy-cured egg yolk. The space is cosy and date-ready – don't bring all your friends.

295 Grand Street, Brooklyn, NY 11211
Nearest station: Metropolitan Avenue
fourhorsemenbk.com

10
AGI'S COUNTER

Dining by the Danube

Eastern European food doesn't normally attract the attention of young chefs, but Jeremy Salamon has taken on the calling with gusto. Named after his nearly 100-year-old Hungarian grandmother Agi, this neighbourhood restaurant steadily turns out dishes worth crossing the East River for. Everything punches above its weight: Caesar salad is remade with bitter radicchio and caraway, rich chicken liver mousse is swished onto griddled bread and dressed in cherry caramel and their cheesecake is lush, tangy and plated on a shallow pool of olive oil. Open five days a week, lunch before or after a visit to the nearby Brooklyn Botanic Garden (no.37) is a classic combo.

818 Franklin Avenue, Brooklyn, NY 11225
Nearest station: Franklin Avenue–Medgar Evers College
agiscounter.com

11

CERVO'S

Portugal's coastline meets Downtown energy

Billing themselves as 'a downtown ode to the seafood of the Iberian Peninsula', Cervo's might sound calm and soothing, but it retains a distinctly New York vibe. The long, lean space pulses with energy emanating from the bustling kitchen and bar at its heart. The bartenders turn out an exceptional 50/50 martini with an olive and lemon peel, and dishes like Montauk red shrimp a la plancha (griddled) showered with Aleppo pepper and Urfa chilli, crispy shrimp heads and salads are consistently beautiful, balanced and bright. Come on a warm evening when the street is blocked off to traffic, making the eastern stretch of Canal Street feel like a summer street party.

43 Canal Street, New York, NY 10002
Nearest station: East Broadway
cervosnyc.com

12

ATOBOY

Korean tasting menu at a steal

Korean cooking is finally having its moment in the sun here, largely due to Hand Hospitality's many ventures and collaborations, including with husband-wife duo Junghyun and Ellia Park at ATOBOY. Behind the spare concrete and wooden facade just north of Koreatown's epicentre, the chefs keep the atmosphere relaxed but the cooking exhilarating. The four-course, $75 seasonal tasting menu often starts with steamed eggs and sea urchin. From there, choose your own adventure with sweet shrimp and white kimchi in beurre blanc or crispy fried squash with Fontina sauce. Their signature Korean fried chicken is available as an add on – a strong move if you're feeling famished.

43 East 28th Street, New York, NY 10016
Nearest station: 28th Street (6)
atoboynyc.com

13

SEMMA

Fiery South Indian flavours

The group that owns this Michelin-starred South Indian restaurant call themselves Unapologetic Foods, and they're true to their moniker. This isn't somewhere servers will ask you how spicy or mild you want your dish served – and they shouldn't. Chef Vijaya Kumar's flavours are bold, bright and don't hold back in the slightest. The immense, triangular gunpowder dosa with potato masala arrives bigger than the plate it's presented on, and the sauce for the valiya chemmeen moilee (Keralan seafood curry, here made with lobster tail, mustard, turmeric and coconut) is rich and seductive. You will need to be tenacious to score a reservation here, but it's well worth seeking out.

60 Greenwich Avenue, New York, NY 10011
Nearest station: 14th Street (F/M)
semma.nyc

14

SUPERIORITY BURGER

Inventive vegetarian cuisine

Individualism has always been this city's core brand, and it's on full display at Superiority Burger. At first blush it looks a bit like a regular diner (and in fact was home to a Ukrainian one for years), but this is one of the city's most surprising restaurants. Chef Brooks Headley's menu is quietly and entirely vegetarian, with lots of vegan options to boot. Most of the dishes come as single items – a braised collard greens sandwich on focaccia, or TFT (tofu fried tofu) on a bun – so order several for the table. Headley was a longtime pastry chef, and desserts like passion fruit pie with tapioca pearls and homemade gelato get as much love from the kitchen as the savoury signatures.

119 Avenue A, New York, NY 10009
Nearest station: Astor Place
superiorityburger.com

15
S&P LUNCH

Old-school counter

The classic New York lunch counter is a dying breed. These are places where anyone can eat, no one will bother you and where you will feel, unmistakably, like you are in the heart of NYC. Across from the Flatiron Building, S&P Lunch marches forward with that tradition. By midday, a lengthy line forms – sometimes right out the door – with folks patiently waiting for a pastrami Reuben, a tuna melt or a cream cheese and olive sandwich that enjoys a cult following. Breakfast, meanwhile, is a quieter affair. Construction and office workers stop in for coffee to go, but grab a seat at the counter for a no-frills plate of eggs or pancakes that will set you up for the whole day.

174 5th Avenue, New York, NY 10010
Nearest station: 23rd Street (R/W)
sandwich.place

16

NEPALI BHANCHHA GHAR

Unmatched momos under the railway tracks

Nepali Bhanchha Ghar is located just below the busting tracks of Jackson Heights station, where several subways and communities converge. We should be grateful there are so many ways to reach their momos. A cornerstone of Tibetan and Nepalese cuisines, the plump, freshly made dumplings are available either fried or steamed, but the jhol rendition, which dances on the edge of being soup and features momos swimming in a rich and heady tomato chutney, is the best thing on the menu. It's good practice to begin with a plate of lafing, a chewy crepe laced with crunchy noodles, chilli and coriander, to prepare for the delights to come.

74–15 Roosevelt Avenue, Queens, NY 11372
Nearest station: Jackson Heights–Roosevelt Avenue
instagram.com/bhanchhaghar

17

SCARR'S PIZZA

A lovingly crafted slice

With so many options at hand and endless debate over the 'best', getting a grip on the city's pizza scene can take time, but owner Scarr Pimentel of Scarr's Pizza is an exceptional guide. Training at the hallowed pizzerias of Lombardi's, Joe's and Artichoke, when Pimentel opened his own joint he applied a level of care rarely seen in the slice world. Milling their own flour on-site, his team turn out both delicate thin-crust pies and thicker Sicilian ones, keeping toppings classic – with a few exceptions like the Hot Boi, dished up with pepperoni, jalapenos and lashings of hot honey. If you're committing to a whole pie, try to score a table in the retro-inspired dining room where you can play an arcade game or two while you wait.

35 Orchard Street, New York, NY 10002
Nearest station: East Broadway
scarrspizza.com

18

RED HOOK TAVERN

NYC's best burger

Known for his devotion to smoked meats, Billy Durney is the man behind this highly inviting tavern serving one of the best burgers in the city. Properly salt and peppered, it's topped with sweet white onion (which also protects the bun from getting soggy) and perfectly melted American cheese. If it's been a long day, start with the very strong Dukes Martini (with overproof gin and vodka), quickly followed by the romaine wedge salad, dressed with tangy pickled mustard seeds, crunchy sourdough crumbs and blue cheese – and last but not least, a thick slab of Nueske's applewood-smoked bacon. Without a reservation, your best bet is to try to walk in for a lazy Friday lunch.

329 Van Brunt Street, Brooklyn, NY 11231
Nearest station: Smith–9th Street
redhooktavern.com

19

TÉ COMPANY

Taiwanese tea oasis

Look out for the minute wooden sign with a kettle etched onto it, or you could easily miss the best Taiwanese tearoom in the city. Tucked away on the first floor of an apartment building, Té has been serving exceptional tea since 2012 – all sourced directly from small-scale farmers in Taiwan. Opt in for petite treats on the side, including their salted yolk mooncake and a pineapple Linzer that is a contender for New York's #1 cookie. Té is best enjoyed at one of the limited in-house tables – there are no reservations, so be prepared to wait if you visit at the weekend. Arrive early, add your name to their waitlist and explore the nearby Jefferson Market Garden, which bursts into a multicoloured spectacle of tulips every spring.

163 W 10th Street, New York, NY 10014
Nearest station: Christopher Street–Stonewall
tecompanytea.com

20

GAGE & TOLLNER

Landmark steakhouse

Gage & Tollner has been serving Brooklynites – almost continuously – since the Gilded Age of the late 19th century. This is the place to order a medium-rare steak served with an entire head of garlic, rich and pillowy rolls, a wedge salad with candied bacon and a perfect dirty martini. The first incarnation opened nearby in 1879, and served until Valentine's Day 2004. After more than a decade of lost years when it was home to an Arby's and a shop selling cell phone cases, it was revived in 2021 – and thank goodness. The brass chandeliers and wooden arches are original, so dining here feels like stepping back into an older, more glamorous New York.

372 Fulton Street, Brooklyn, NY 11201 ·
Nearest station: Jay Street–MetroTech
gageandtollner.com

21

RAKU

Udon specialists at work

Chef Norihiro Ishizuka started his udon-making career when he was 13. More than 60 years later, his East Village institution turns out seemingly bottomless bowls of chewy udon noodles in steaming broth, with additions like oysters or light vegetable tempura served on the side (so you can gradually add it to the mix while it remains crisp). The indoor space is tiny and sparsely decorated, packing in diners like sardines, but an outdoor dining space that opened during the pandemic has joyfully provided a covert expansion of the seats on offer. There's little on the menu besides udon, so come for noodles, or don't come at all.

342 East 6th Street, New York, NY 10003
Nearest station: Astor Place or 2nd Avenue
Other locations: SoHo, Midtown
rakunyc.com

22

AUNTS ET UNCLES

Plant-based Caribbean fare

This cafe-restaurant-shop is run by husband-and-wife team Mike and Nicole Nicholas and feels closer to your cool aunt's home, complete with houseplants and books. While many of Michael's peers left to seek success outside of this Caribbean corner of Flatbush, the duo chose to invest in the community – and it's all the better for it. A plant-based menu inspired by their Caribbean roots leads the way: 'fish' cakes are reimagined with hearts of palm, and the Cryin' Ryan – a hunk of cauliflower encrusted with a rich, spicy peanut sauce – is cheekily named for their nephew. If there are any carnivores in your pack, the AU burger with Beyond Meat, caramelised onions and spicy mayo is rich enough to satisfy even the unconverted.

1407 Nostrand Avenue, Brooklyn, NY 11226
Nearest station: Winthrop Street
auntsetuncles.com

23

UN POSTO ITALIANO

Italy, no passport required

Equal parts Italian speciality shop and cafe, Un Posto Italiano flies under the radar but has an exceptionally devoted following among those in the know. Essentially, it feels like stepping onto a patch of Italian soil that just happens to be in Brooklyn. Regulars come for cappuccini in the sunny backyard, fresh pasta to cook at home or the pleasure of speaking Italian with the owners. Arrive early for their sell-out sfogliatella, a flaky cornucopia-shaped pastry filled with orange-laced ricotta. Place an order to collect the house-made pasta by calling them ahead of time – a full day in advance if it's a weekend.

206 Garfield Place, Brooklyn, NY 11215
Nearest station: 7th Avenue
unpostoitaliano.com

24

RADIO BAKERY

Lamination for days

New York is living through a golden age of pastry-making (which started as a silver lining to the pandemic) and Radio Bakery is leading the scene. Owned by the team behind cosy Ridgewood date spot Rolo's, this Greenpoint bakery turns out the classics, but also folds more unexpected options between its flaky offerings, like scallion sesame twists and cheesy pretzel bearclaws. If you find yourself within a five-block radius at lunchtime, make a beeline for their sandwiches, which include combinations like burrata, prosciutto and basil, all squeezed between two life-affirming slabs of focaccia. The lines are legendary, but Radio is worth waiting for. Patience, your triple chocolate croissant is coming.

135 India Street, Brooklyn, NY 11222
Nearest station: Greenpoint Avenue
radiobakery.nyc

25

POPUP BAGELS

Hot property baked goods

Here's a secret: the best bagel in New York is normally the best bagel within walking distance of wherever in the city you've woken up. Any self-respecting bagel shop in the city will serve fresh bagels with an acceptable level of chew and an optional topping. But if you're the kind of person willing to move mountains for the most coveted bagels of the moment, proceed directly to PopUp Bagels in Greenwich Village. Here, they are served hot from the oven and the schmear (spread) comes on the side for dunking. Beware! They enforce a controversial 3 bagels + 1 schmear minimum. Take your loot to Washington Square Park (no.42) for some world-class people-watching – from chess players to protestors, the possibilities are endless.

177 Thompson Street, New York, NY 10012
Nearest station: Spring Street (C/E)
Other locations: Upper East Side, Upper West Side
popupbagels.com

26

SEY COFFEE

Superb coffee and peak Bushwick fashion

Caffeine fiends with sharp eyes may spot SEY's sleek square boxes of beans at cafes like Villager in Crown Heights, but they are best prepared at the team's roastery and airy cafe in Bushwick. Options like the Franci Elena come with tasting notes detailing citrus, lychee and raspberry, and list the origin country of the beans. Order your jolt to stay and it will be presented on a wooden board alongside a glass of seltzer. No laptops are permitted on the weekends, but don't worry – the people-watching is unmissable: think 'straight out of central casting' with a Bushwick aesthetic, complete with intentionally wildly mismatched outfits.

18 Grattan Street, Brooklyn, NY 11206
Nearest station: Morgan Avenue
seycoffee.com

27
LYSÉE

Paean to the pastry

Tracing a path from Korea to the pastry schools of France, Eunji Lee's exquisite confections are crafted at a level you would expect from a multi-Michelin-starred team. Individual pastries are displayed on the upstairs floor like artworks, prompting reverent hushed tones from customers. In the slightly more lively downstairs dining room, Lee offers a tasting menu, brunch and a la carte options. The corn mousse cake with sablé (shortbread) and grilled corn cream is highly coveted, but the more gently priced viennoiserie – a chocolate babka with a shatteringly crisp shell, and the flaky kouign-amann with a buttery, caramelised bottom – will blow you away. The madeleine offerings change seasonally, but if the black sesame cream-filled ones are on offer, don't leave without them.

44 E 21st Street, NY 10010
Nearest station: 23rd Street (6)
lyseenyc.com

28
COURT
STREET GROCERS

The sandwich kings of New York City

From chopped cheese in the Bronx to pastrami on the Lower East Side and the ubiquitous BEC (bacon, egg and cheese) at countless bodegas around the city, New Yorkers take sandwiches seriously. This zeal is on full display at Court Street Grocers, owned by Eric Finkelstein and Matt Ross, who also operate S&P (no.15). You're in capable hands here, with a menu that includes a standout Reuben Brocc (roasted broccoli, Swiss cheese and sauerkraut) and the Ultimate Warrior (pork shoulder, broccoli rabe, provolone, pecorino and pickled pepper). The Vegitalian, which swaps cured meat for roasted sweet potato then pairs it with three cheeses and a briny house spread, has diehard fans for a reason.

485 Court Street, Brooklyn, NY 11231
Nearest station: Smith–9th Street
Other locations: Williamsburg, Greenwich Village
courtstreetgrocers.com

29

OTWAY BAKERY

Beautifully burnished buns

Samantha Safer is a hands-on restaurateur; you can usually find her dusted with flour in the kitchen, carefully shaping cardamom buns or loaves of sourdough bread. In addition to baguettes that perfectly balance a crispy exterior with chewy interior and pastéis de nata filled with golden custard, you might stumble upon specials here like pan Suisse buns with malted rye frangipane and sour cherries. You're also likely to find long lines of neighbours and the city's pastry fiends eagerly waiting their turn to ponder the day's selection. Most of the space is dedicated to baking rather than sitting, so consider taking your haul to nearby Fort Greene or Prospect Park.

920a Fulton Street, Brooklyn, NY 11238
Nearest station: Clinton–Washington Avenues (C)
instagram.com/otwaybakery

30
PAMINA
DOLCI & GELATO

Italy-meets-NYC in a scoop

The rich and wonderfully creamy gelato on this unassuming stretch of 6th Avenue should be a reminder to all of us that gelato need not be inhibited by unhelpful social norms – like whether it happens to be mid-winter, or whether you had a scoop a few hours ago. Pamina keeps their options simple with classics like lemon sorbet, peach and hazelnut, made with fruit from the Union Square Greenmarket (no.45) and Italian delicacies including Piemonte hazelnuts. If you're an avid cook, pop into Travelers Poets & Friends, the cafe–bakery next door owned by the same team, offering an extended selection of pasta and provisions.

457 6th Avenue, New York, NY 10011
Nearest station: 14th Street (F/M)
paminadolcegelato.com

31
BURROW

Exquisite and unusual bakes

Burrow is hard to find; there is no clear signage and the bakery is set back in the lobby of a large building. To add to the challenge, it's only open four days a week for a few hours at a time – and none of those days are over the weekend. But none of that matters when the baking is this good. Once you locate Burrow, you might be greeted by custardy canelès, mocha biscuit coffee cakes and crisp apple galettes topped with paper-thin slices of fruit or caramel buttercream. Take your bounty to the East River for a view of Manhattan and the bridges – just know the pastries are likely to command your attention.

68 Jay Street #119, Brooklyn, NY 11201
Nearest station: York Street
burrow.nyc

32

TATIANA BY KWAME ONWUACHI

Afro-Caribbean food with a side of performing arts

Restaurants at arts institutions rarely measure up to the art. That's not the case at Tatiana by Kwame Onwuachi. With the exceptionally talented Onwuachi leading the kitchen, this restaurant in Lincoln Center (no.85) tells compelling stories through its cuisine. Drawing on his West African, Caribbean and Bronx heritage, Onwuachi serves dishes like dumplings filled with crab and egusi (a kind of gourd) soup, and a short rib pastrami suya with caraway coco bread. The only choice you have is between the 'small share' and 'large share' menu, so leave picky eaters at home. The restaurant is loud and lively; save your deep conversations for a post-dinner stroll around Lincoln Center Plaza. You could go before or after a show, but Tatiana is a main event.

10 Lincoln Center Plaza, New York, NY 10023
Nearest station: 66 Street–Lincoln Centre
tatiananyc.com

33
UNA PIZZA
NAPOLETANA

A hell of a lot cheaper than a flight to Naples

If you want to eat the best Neapolitan-style pizza in the city, you will do so on acclaimed pizzaiolo Anthony Mangieri's terms. The New Jersey native operates his Lower East Side pizzeria three nights a week: Thursday, Friday and Saturday. Working exclusively with Italian flours, naturally leavened dough is shaped at a glass-fronted station before being charred to perfection in the wood-fired oven. Options are limited: five classics including a marinara and an excellent margherita with pillows of melted mozzarella, plus one special a week. Reservations are practically mandatory, but you could try to score one of the scarce walk-in spots by lining up around 4:30pm and saying a quick prayer to the Madonna that stands guard atop the bar.

175 Orchard Street, New York, NY 10002
Nearest station: 2nd Avenue
unapizza.com

34

VALENTINO PIER

A sight of New York's most famous silhouette

This pier at the edge of Red Hook gives you an up close and personal look at the Statue of Liberty – she faces the pier almost head on. A gift from France, Lady Liberty has welcomed countless ships in New York Harbor since she was installed on what's now known as Liberty Island in 1886. Both she and the view into New York Harbor look best around sunset, so plan an early evening visit. Know this: there are no subway stops near Valentino Pier, but it's a trek worth making. The best way to get there is by Citi Bike from Brooklyn Bridge Park (see no.38) or by car. Try to snag a table at Red Hook Tavern (see no.18) for dinner while you're in the neighbourhood.

Ferris Street &, Coffey Street, Brooklyn, NY 11231
Nearest station: Smith–9th Street
nycgovparks.org/parks/valentino-pier

35

CENTRAL PARK

Urban mega oasis

Central Park provides vital respite from the swarms of high rises, yellow taxis and hot dog vendors that make up the glorious chaos of Manhattan. At 843 acres, it's vast, and best enjoyed on a long ramble. The Mall & Literary Walk is shaded by majestically large elm trees, then there's the awe-inspiring Bethesda Fountain with its towering *Angel of the Waters* sculpture and the lake. Hop by the White Rabbit at the Alice in Wonderland sculpture on your way out by the Met (no.66). Alternatively, enter on the west side by the 'Imagine' mosaic at Strawberry Fields to explore the lush Shakespeare Gardens and follow the path to Belvedere Castle.

New York, NY
centralparknyc.org

36

PROSPECT PARK

Brooklyn's backyard

Designed by pioneering American landscape architect Frederick Law Olmsted and the lesser known Calvert Vaux (the same dynamic duo behind Central Park, no.35), Prospect Park is every Brooklynite's backyard. Bike, run or walk the 3.35-mile loop on a sunny weekend and you will see members of many communities that call Brooklyn home: Caribbean, Latinx and Orthodox Jewish families, the stroller set from nearby Park Slope and groups of 20-somethings. Barbecuing, picnicking, sunbathing, slacklining – anything goes. On Saturdays, swing by the Grand Army Plaza Greenmarket at the northern tip of the park for a snack or picnic provisions.

Brooklyn, NY
Nearest station: Grand Army Plaza
prospectpark.org

37

BROOKLYN BOTANIC GARDEN

Cherry blossom mania

Located just beside Prospect Park (no.36) and the Brooklyn Museum, Brooklyn's Botanic Garden is smaller than the New York Botanic Garden in the Bronx but is still utterly delightful and certainly easier to get to. The Italian-style Osborne Garden with multihued rhododendron and the Japanese Hill-and-Pond Garden with its koi fish are transportive, but it's the Cherry Esplanade that draws New Yorkers every spring. The park's team provides regular updates via CherryWatch, an online map neatly detailing what stage of bloom each cherry tree is at. Around the holidays, the Lightscape transforms the park after dark, with over one million lights.

150 Eastern Parkway, Brooklyn, NY 11225
Nearest station: Botanic Garden
Other entrances at: 455 Flatbush Avenue,
990 Washington Avenue
bbg.org

38

BROOKLYN BRIDGE PARK

Sprawling green space by an iconic bridge

Hugging the Brooklyn side of the East River, this 85-acre park boasts some of the best views of the Manhattan skyline that the city has to offer, across six brilliantly designed piers. It's hard to imagine such a green spot in one of the world's most frenzied cities, but the staggering views are especially well complemented by picnics and ice cream. Wooded and grassy areas on Piers 1, 6 and 3 offer quiet respite from the city, while the rink (skates in the summer, blades in the winter) on Pier 2 and the football pitch on Pier 5 are ideal if you have some extra energy to burn. On hot summer evenings, stop off for a drink on Pilot, the swanky sailboat–bar that docks at Pier 6.

Brooklyn waterfront from Dumbo to Atlantic Avenue
brooklynbridgepark.org

39
BROOKLYN BRIDGE

Awe-inspiring views over the East River

An outing to a bridge? It might not sound that thrilling, but locals and visitors have been strolling across this suspension bridge between Brooklyn and Manhattan since 1883. (Circus founder P.T. Barnum also famously walked 21 elephants and 17 camels across it in 1884 to prove its strength.) Even the most jaded New Yorker cannot deny the dazzling views of the Manhattan and Brooklyn skylines, with New York Harbour in particular coming alive at sunset. Walk from Brooklyn to Manhattan, turn north at City Hall and head to Chinatown for dinner, or pack a picnic and set out from City Hall to find a spot in Brooklyn Bridge Park (see no.38).

Brooklyn Bridge, New York and Brooklyn
Nearest station: Brooklyn Bridge–City Hall or High Street

40
HIGH LINE

Railway line reborn

This narrow, 1.45-mile long greenway on the far West Side of Manhattan is one of the city's most beautifully designed public spaces. It's made even more remarkable by its history: built as an elevated freight train line in the 1930s, the space sat empty for decades and was nearly demolished before local conservationists saved it. Today, the park runs from the glossy mall at Hudson Yards down to The Whitney (no.68). While various artworks dot the walkway, it's the views, design and landscaping (there are 500+ species of plants and trees here) that are the real draw. The elevated vantage point affords a rare view down bustling 23rd Street and, in spring, the Redbud blossoms are spectacular.

New York, NY 10011
Nearest station: 34th Street–Hudson Yards
thehighline.org

41

RIEGELMANN BOARDWALK

Sea breezes, kitsch and Russian fare

Better known as the Coney Island Boardwalk, this wooden walkway runs nearly three miles along Brooklyn's beachfront. New York isn't exactly a beach destination and there are certainly purer sands to be found elsewhere, but the boardwalk's charms are undeniable. Start in Coney Island and visit Luna Park for rides like the iconic wooden roller coaster The Cyclone, then continue down to Brighton Beach, a neighbourhood many immigrants from the former Soviet Union call home. Set course for the comically large spread at Tashkent Supermarket – think Russian salads, Uzbek plov, towering slices of honey cake – and return to a bench on the boardwalk to dine in style.

Riegelmann Boardwalk, Brooklyn, NY
Nearest station: West 8th Street–New York Aquarium
nycgovparks.org/parks/coney-island-beach-and-boardwalk

42

WASHINGTON SQUARE PARK

New York's most New York park

There are parks you visit for beauty, but Washington Square in the heart of Greenwich Village isn't one of them. Sure, the arch is iconic and the fountain is nice, but New Yorkers gravitate here because there's always something happening, whether that's heated chess games or lively protests. Mix in gaggles of NYU students hanging out between classes and musicians of varying skill levels playing for cash, and you get the idea. Show up anytime and see what's doing. The scene is best enjoyed with a bagel from nearby PopUp Bagels (see no.25) and a coffee.

Washington Square, New York, NY 10012
Nearest station: West Fourth Street–Washington Square
nycgovparks.org/parks/washington-square-park

43

HUDSON RIVER GREENWAY

Roll down Manhattan on a bike

Stretching nearly the entire length of Manhattan's West Side, the Hudson River Greenway (part of the larger Manhattan Waterfront Greenway) gives cyclists and pedestrians desperately needed respite from the city's crushing traffic congestion and a breeze from the Hudson River. Make your way up or down the island, stopping at foodhall Market 57 and Little Island, a park that sits on tulip-shaped stilts rising up from the water. You'll cover more ground with a bicycle, and Citi Bike conveniently has plenty of docking stations with both regular and e-bikes scattered around – helmets aren't provided, so ride carefully.

Chambers Street, New York, NY 10006
Nearest station: Chambers Street (1/2/3)

44

FRANKLIN D. ROOSEVELT FOUR FREEDOMS STATE PARK

Meditative moment on the East River

Roosevelt Island sits in the middle of the East River but feels entirely distinct from the city. Located at the southern tip beside the ivy-covered ruins of a 19th-century smallpox hospital, this riverside state park is an uncannily quiet, all-enveloping monument to the longest serving US president. Ascend the stairs to a triangular-shaped, tree-lined lawn whose shaded walkways converge towards an enormous floating bust of Roosevelt and, behind him, a view of the United Nations. The journey to the island (by subway, ferry or car) is part of its charm. If heights thrill you, catch the tram over the East River from the Manhattan side.

1 FDR Four Freedoms Park, New York, NY 10044
Nearest station: Roosevelt Island
fdrfourfreedomspark.org

45

UNION SQUARE GREENMARKET

Best produce in the city

Starting life as a homespun local market selling goods from a few farmers back in 1976, the
Union Square Greenmarket has since grown
into a sprawling affair with the biggest and the
best range of produce in the city. Set a pre-dawn
alarm on Wednesdays to pick out the most desirable goods (the Korean cucumbers at Lani's are
breathtakingly crunchy) or stroll through on a
sunny Saturday if you prefer savouring the ambi-
ance – just brace yourself for the inevitable crowds
seeking artisan pickles and rainbow carrots. Some
parting advice: while the market's baked treats are
good, the pastries at Breads Bakery, half a block
away, are better.

Union Square, New York, NY 10003
Nearest station: 14th Street–Union Square
grownyc.org/greenmarket/manhattan-union-square-m

46
MCNALLY JACKSON BOOKS

NYC's favourite neighbourhood bookstore

For years, McNally Jackson stood as a singular, beloved independent bookstore on Prince Street in SoHo. While many indie booksellers had difficulty grappling with the rise of Amazon and later the global pandemic, McNally Jackson cleared both hurdles and flourished. It showcases a thoughtful fiction display and stellar cookbook selection curated by writer Cheryl Pearl Sucher, but it's the periodicals that make the shop so unique. Alongside magazine stand mainstays are jewels like *Yolo Journal* for travel junkies and the climate-driven *Icarus Complex*. The chainlet now operates five stores, with two in Brooklyn and three in Manhattan, running regular activities for little ones and hot-ticket author talks at their Seaport location, as well as poetry readings.

134 Prince St, New York, NY 10012
Nearest station: Spring Street (C/E)
Other locations: multiple, see website
mcnallyjackson.com

47

MOMA DESIGN STORE

A museum gift shop that's leagues apart

The MoMA Design Store isn't your typical museum gift shop hawking fusty silk scarves. Yes, there are art books and posters – particularly at the Midtown location across the street from the museum – but this store offers much, much more. Everything is painstakingly reviewed by the museum's curators, from delicate, accordion-shaped folding bags by Issey Miyake to neon signs that take their cue from the paintings of Jean-Michel Basquiat. Among the selection are exclusive items, including illustrated wooden trays by artist Yoshitomo Nara, whose manga-inspired images of scowling children form part of the museum's collection.

44 West 53rd Street, New York, NY 10019
Nearest station: 5th Avenue–53rd Street
Other locations: SoHo
store.moma.org

48

KALUSTYAN'S

A paradise of spice

The team at Kalustyan's call their 80-year-old shop 'A Landmark for Fine Specialty Foods'. This is no throwaway puffery; it's the go-to shopping spot for countless chefs and cooks in the city. Devotees come in their droves to wander Kalustyan's neatly stacked shelves, parading a dizzyingly vast selection of spices and delicacies, from lion's mane mushroom powder and pulverised red seaweed to Chinese black rice, all crowned by a wall of hot sauces and fruit-flavoured sugars in neon hues. Not unlike the Met (see no.66), you're always guaranteed to unearth something new here.

123 Lexington Avenue, New York, NY 10016
Nearest station: 28th Street (6)
foodsofnations.com

49

COMING SOON

Chromatic homeware

Located in what's now known as Dimes Square (a much-memed corner of the Lower East Side), Coming Soon is one the city's most vibrantly hued homeware and gift shops. Pieces like the Third Drawer Down corn stool might already be lodged in your visual recall and the pantone-striped towels from Brooklyn's Dusen Dusen may already be at the top of your not-so-secret wishlist, but part of the joy of shopping here is taking in the kitschy visual cacophony in a space that feels somewhere between a showroom and an eclectic friend's home. While stock includes a number of splurge items (that corn stool is a cool $275), much of the selection is within easier reach.

53 Canal St, New York, NY 10002
Nearest station: East Broadway
comingsoonnewyork.com

50
WRAY

Fashion for every body

Inclusive fashion has (thankfully) taken some giant leaps forward in recent years. A prime example of this is Lower East Side fashion brand Wray, which is truly for every *body*, no matter your size, race, age, gender identity or expression. Founded by Wray Serna, who cut her teeth at Issey Miyake and Rachel Comey, the clothing comes in sizes XXS through to 6X, with friendly staff happy to help with sizing and styling. The light-filled boutique is dominated by bright colours and bold prints, but there's plenty of black apparel, too – this is New York, after all – and all the garments are made in fair-trade facilities. If you're looking for even more size-inclusive fashion, Big Bud Press is just up Orchard Street.

38 Orchard Street, New York, NY 10002
Nearest station: East Broadway
wray.nyc

51

OPEN INVITE

Indie design meets vintage homeware

Brooklyn's Red Hook neighbourhood is somehow both quintessentially New York and simultaneously entirely on its own planet; it's gritty, artsy and moves to its own beat. This is vividly apparent at Open Invite, which stocks both a desirable selection of homeware from indie brands – think eye-catching tumblers from Yield and cheese knives from Fredericks & Mae – alongside unique, vintage radish-shaped ceramics and one-of-a-kind green mid-century glass vases. With breweries and chocolate factories vying for space and a revolving door of artists, makers and writers, this corner of Brooklyn has an undeniable gravitational force.

317 Van Brunt Street, Brooklyn, NY 11231
Nearest station: Smith–9th Street
openinviteshop.com

52
50 NORMAN

Tokyo story

Behind a wall of windows on Greenpoint's Norman Street sits a sprawling space built with wood from demolished houses in Kyoto. Finished with pale grey floors, it's calm and inviting, even when there's a crowd. The space hosts three Japanese businesses: House, an elevated Japanese-French restaurant tucked away during the day behind retractable wooden walls, veteran dashi company Dashi Okume and Cibone, offering a well-curated selection of artisanal home goods plus chic leather bags from Hender Scheme. Visit during lunchtime and treat yourself to a set meal with tea, rice, fish, miso and Japanese pickles. Don't depart without designing your own custom dashi mix for home at Dashi Okume.

50 Norman Avenue, Brooklyn, NY 11222
Nearest station: Nassau Avenue
50norman.com

Custom-made Dashi Stand

Step 1

Select one ingredient
from each category
based on
our golden ratio
[A:50% B:30% C:10% D:10%]

A Dried fish
[Inosinic acid]

+ B Dried small fish
[Inosinic acid]

+ D Mushrooms
[Guanylic acid]

or Others
[Distin

Step 2
Ingredients are
blended and packed

Step 3
Your original dashi
is complete

Vegetable dashi
can also be
made to order

53

JOHN DERIAN

A designer's 2nd street empire

The lush world of John Derian stretches across three storefronts in the East Village, and is packed to the gills with beautiful objects. Start at the decoupage trays and plates that catapulted John Derian to fame. Alongside these sit candles from Italian company Cereria Introna, convincingly shaped as large wedges of cake and cheese. Move on to the furniture showroom one door down, which is filled with antiques (and the odd 19th-century bicycle), before entering textile fantasyland, with the added delight of perfumes by Parisian brand Astier de Villatte. Throughout the shop, fanciful lamps and hand-blown glass mobiles by Julia Condon command admiration.

6 East 2nd Street, New York, NY 10003
Nearest station: 2nd Avenue
johnderian.com

SHOPS

54

BERGDORF GOODMAN

Luxury fashion worth ogling

If you've ever watched a TV series or a film set in New York featuring any sort of mega-rich person shopping, chances are you've seen Bergdorf Goodman. Located on 5th Avenue next to The Plaza Hotel, it's as glamorous as you might imagine, and every bit as lovely to roam – even if you can't afford a $5,000 dress or $500 bottle of perfume. Much of the store is organised as mini-boutiques dedicated to designers, giving you a peek at this season's lines (and saving you having to race up and down Madison Avenue). Unless you've come for something specific, Bergdorf's is best enjoyed as a fashion museum and, like any good museum, the people-watching is part of the show, so enjoy the parade of wealthy Upper East Siders with children and nannies in tow.

754 5th Avenue, New York, NY 10019
Nearest station: 5th Avenue/59th Street
bergdorfgoodman.com

55

BEAM

Scandinavia-meets-Williamsburg

This Scandi homeware store by Williamsburg's waterfront blends strong colour with whimsy (the little red and white ceramic mushrooms are especially delightful). Pendant lights from British designer Tom Dixon complement kintsugi pottery by Seletti. Strikingly, several walls are lined with works from Wallpaper Projects, and look more like large-scale art pieces than anything so quotidian as wallpaper. Many eras gets representation here, with globular mid-century lamps and iridescent wallpaper behind the checkout counter that looks like a 21st-century take on the Impressionists. If you need time to contemplate your purchase, walk over one block to Domino Park, a six-acre park along the waterfront.

272 Kent Avenue, Brooklyn, NY 11249
Nearest station: Bedford Avenue
beambk.com

56

FRONT GENERAL STORE

Vintage lair in Dumbo

The real joy of vintage shopping is not knowing what you might find, and there's plenty to unearth at this unassuming spot in Dumbo, a Brooklyn neighbourhood at the base of Manhattan Bridge. Cross the threshhold and you'll find yourself knee-deep in vintage Levi's and leather Coach bags, sprinkled with the occasional ceramic soap dish from India and handmade slippers from Morocco. Those with a vintage shopping addiction shouldn't miss the FSG Outpost a few doors down, where you can find covetable couture pieces from houses like Givenchy and Margiela. You're also just around the corner from Burrow bakery (see no.31), if you'd like a s'more tart to top off all that retro nostalgia.

143 Front Street, Brooklyn, NY 11201
Nearest station: York Street
Other location: FSG (Outpost)
frontgeneralstore.com

57

COMMON THINGS

Micro-shop filled with eclectic design

The idea behind architect and designer Komal Kehar's pocket-sized shop reflects Pablo Neruda's *Odes to Common Things*: it is often the most ordinary of things that colour our lives. Kehar's selection is intentionally wide-ranging and story-forward, dotted with objects sourced from her travels. You might find a rooster-shaped watering can, hand-woven hammam towels from Tunisia, bars of olive oil soap from the Palestinian Soap Cooperative or glass goblets with protruding noses, eyes and mouths from Objet Paris. The East Village is a mecca for quirky, small shops like this, with Japanese stationary store niconeco zakkaya and the micro-bakery Lady Wong both close by. Before exploring any further, cross the street to Abraço (see no.8) for an espresso.

76 East 7th Street, New York, NY 10003
Nearest station: Astor Place
common-things.com

58
DASHWOOD BOOKS

Subterranean photography books

Owned by David Strettell, the former cultural director of Magnum, Dashwood is the type of shop that feels classically New York: obsessively niche, a little dusty and, most vitally, a space dedicated to community – in this case, photographers. Sift through and you might find collections of Polaroids by Richard Kern, playful zines filled with amateur web photography or brilliant collections from the 1970s Paris nightclub scene. Since 2008, Dashwood has also published works like *Daido Moriyama Shashin Jidai 1981–1988*, celebrating the trailblazing Japanese photographer. Don't miss a trip to Dashwood Projects, the newly opened experimental exhibition space just a few blocks away.

33 Bond Street, New York, NY 10012
Nearest station: Bleecker Street
dashwoodbooks.com

59

BIG NIGHT

Chic supplies for the ultimate night in

'Not every night is a dinner party kinda night – but any night can be a Big Night', is Katherine Lewin's philosophy. Lewin launched her first shop in Greenpoint in 2021, later opening the considerably larger space in the West Village to offer everything required for a special night in. Vintage coupes and plush pillows shaped like martini olives are flanked by brightly hued bistro kitchenware. What goes on the plate is just as important, with little kitchen luxuries like ice cream from local producers Bad Habit, spices from sustainable brand Diaspora Co. and golden-wrapped roundels of Beurre de Baratte from Normandy, speckled with sea salt. You'll need to make a stop at Union Square Greenmarket (no.45) for produce worthy of your platters.

236 West 10th Street, New York, NY 10014
Nearest station: Christopher Street–Stonewall
Other location: Greenpoint
bignightbk.com

60
HOUSING WORKS BOOKSTORE

Second-hand books and clothes with a mission

Since 1990, Housing Works has supported and advocated for over 30,000 New Yorkers living with and affected by HIV/AIDS and facing homelessness. The organisation's SoHo bookstore, nine vintage stores and dispensary support that vital mission. The first floor of the bookstore includes everything from children's books to fiction and cookbooks, while the mezzanine holds vintage clothes and shoes. The experience is more about discovery than finding a copy of the latest bestseller and, if you want to linger over your purchase, take a seat in the 1990s-feeling cafe at the back. Like a college, free condoms are always available at the check-out counter.

126 Crosby Street, New York, NY 10012
Nearest station: Broadway–Lafayette Street
housingworks.org/locations/bookstore-cafe

61

ABC CARPET & HOME

High-class homeware

Even if hand-knotted $10,000 rugs, $875 woollen llama sculptures and Ginori 1735 porcelain tableware aren't within your price range, this two-storey homeware and carpet shop just north of Union Square is a pleasure to meander through. The displays, which feature dried flowers as well as twigs beautifully woven into what looks like a giant bird's nest, are as impressive as the intriguing rarities for sale. Pretty much everything here feels delicate and highly breakable, so leave any butter-fingered friends at home – or deposit them with your little ones in the nearby playground at Union Square.

888 Broadway, New York, NY 10003
Nearest station: 14th Street–Union Square
abchome.com

62

CASA MAGAZINES

Print mecca

A visit to the West Village isn't complete without stopping at Casa Magazines, one of the city's last old-school shops dedicated to the glossies. Casa has survived thanks in large part to former owner Mohammed Ahmed, who bought the shop in 1994, and a genuinely heartwarming Instagram account which launched with a post of journalist Malcolm Gladwell at the counter. In its compact West Village corner, Casa stocks thousands of rare mags – seemingly every international edition of *Vogue* is here, alongside car aficionado mag *Evo*, the elevated pages of *Architectural Digest France* and queer magazine *Kink*. Longtime co-worker Syed Khalid Wasim (known to regulars as Ali) has recently taken over, with Casa remaining a beloved neighbourhood landmark.

22 8th Avenue, New York, NY 10014
Nearest station: 14th Street (A/C/E/L)
instagram.com/casamagazinesnyc

63

STRAND BOOKSTORE

New York's (unofficial) bookstore

When 25-year-old Ben Bass opened the Strand in 1927 with $600, it was part of 'Book Row' – one of 48 bookstores spread across six blocks. Tragically, those days are long gone, but the Strand's four floors just south of Union Square are a permanent city fixture. The vast selection covers everything from world history to Black art – navigate the new, used and rare books using the many display tables as your guide. Each has a helpful maroon sign, some obvious ('Bestsellers') and others a bit more niche ('Curated by The Metropolitan Opera'). Grab one of the shop's totes emblazoned with their slogan – '18 miles of books' – to carry your latest acquisition, and crack the spine on your next subway ride.

828 Broadway, New York, NY 10003
Nearest station: 14th Street–Union Square
strandbooks.com

64
THE MORGAN LIBRARY & MUSEUM

The life and libraries of the rich and famous

Ornate Renaissance-style rooms may provide the initial lure, but it's the works from J. Pierpont Morgan's personal library that will really stagger you. Continually expanding since the 1900s, the illustrious collection includes a pocket-sized memorandum book belonging to Sir Isaac Newton, a copy of the Declaration of Independence (one of only 25 in existence), compositions by Bach and Mozart and three copies of the Gutenberg Bible (because one is never enough). Previous exhibitions have spotlighted the endearing animals of Beatrix Potter or taken deep dives into Franz Kafka's manuscripts, photos and correspondence. Catch live music (and free entry) on Fridays from 5–7pm.

225 Madison Avenue, New York, NY 10016
Nearest station: 33rd Street
themorgan.org

65

THE ROSE MAIN
READING ROOM, NYPL

Majestic study space in New York's public library

The New York Public Library is a vital and beloved resource that keeps New Yorkers of all ages reading and offers city dwellers quiet respite (and a bathroom) when most needed. Its crown jewel is the Rose Main Reading Room at the Stephen A. Schwarzman Building in Bryant Park. The serene, 297-foot-long room has arched windows, with natural light streaming in to illuminate a majestic, gilded ceiling. If you just want to look around, you will need to join a tour or come in the mornings (check their website), but anyone is welcome to use the space for research, writing or reading. Pull up one of the wooden chairs at the long tables and gaze up at the painted blue skies on the ceiling between pages.

476 5th Avenue, New York, NY 10018
Nearest station: 5th Avenue
nypl.org

66

THE METROPOLITAN MUSEUM OF ART

The grand dame of the art world

No matter how many times you visit, there's always more to marvel at in the Met. You might find yourself in an exhibition from the Costume Institute, tagging along on a tour of the jaw-dropping Impressionist galleries or gawping at the Egyptian Temple of Dendur that dates back to 15BCE, but now resides in the Upper East Side. There's an extensive roster of expert talks, artist-led tours and interactive sessions for kids, exploring works in the decorative arts or the Harlem Renaissance as well as topics in art from spirituality, fashion and music. If you're ever feeling overwhelmed by the crowds, claim a seat under the sprawling skylight in the Greek and Roman gallery to recharge.

1000 5th Ave, New York, NY 10028
Nearest station: 77th Street
metropolitanmuseum.org

67

TENEMENT MUSEUM

New York: living on top of one another

With the boutiques, tiny art galleries and shiny relocated Essex Market (no.6) now populating the Lower East Side, it's easy to forget how different these streets looked a century or two ago. Back then, they were bustling with Irish, Jewish, German, Italian and Black migrant families – all looking to find their way in the city. Seven thousand of these new arrivals called 97 Orchard Street home. Today, you can sign up for a tour to step into their recreated apartments and learn about how they lived, worked, worshipped and settled into New York life.

103 Orchard Street, New York, NY 10002
Nearest station: Delancey Street–Essex Street
tenement.org

THE WHITNEY MUSEUM OF AMERICAN ART

Art and architecture in harmony

Two years after sculptor Gertrude Vanderbilt Whitney's collection was turned down by the Met (no.66) in 1929, she opened the first iteration of The Whitney. The permanent collection – including Alexander Calder's bright kinetic sculptures, the proto-Pop Art of Jasper Johns and Georgia O'Keeffe's sensuous natural forms – is complemented by rotating exhibitions and the museum's flagship biennial. The asymmetrically stacked building by Renzo Piano sports terraces with views of the city skyline and an outpost of the celebrated Frenchette Bakery. It is in itself a work of art that perfectly compliments both its collection and it's immediate neighbourhood – the Meatpacking District.

99 Gansevoort Street, New York, NY 10014
Nearest station: 14th Street (A/C/E/L)
whitney.org

69

COOPER HEWITT, SMITHSONIAN DESIGN MUSEUM

Refined design museum

Museum Mile stretches along the northeastern side of Central Park right up 5th Avenue, and is so densely packed with blockbusters like the Met (see no.66) and the Guggenheim, one could easily overlook smaller gems like Cooper Hewitt. That would be a mistake. The only American museum dedicated solely to contemporary and historical design, the collection ranges from vintage radios to office chairs, historic textiles and porcelain tea cups. Housed in Andrew Carnegie's fin-de-siècle mansion, parquet floors and carved ceilings are a prelude to the capacious garden now serving as a public park. Don't miss their design-focused shop for stylish homeware, books and gifts.

2 E 91st Street, New York, NY 10128
Nearest station: 96th Street (6)
cooperhewitt.org

70

JUDD FOUNDATION

Artist's home frozen in time

Artist Donald Judd's meticulously preserved and renovated home in SoHo – which he referred to as 'permanent installation' – is a reflection of how space can inform artistic work. Built in 1870 to house several small factories, Judd purchased all five floors of the cast-iron building in 1968, back when urban planner Robert Moses was threatening to install a highway across SoHo. Join a tour to admire the decorative objects and textiles set against the bright, warm wood of Judd's rooms, alongside his own artwork and those of artists including Marcel Duchamp, Jean Arp and Larry Bell.

101 Spring St, New York, NY 10012
Nearest station: Spring Street (6)
juddfoundation.org/visit/new-york

71

INTERNATIONAL CENTER OF PHOTOGRAPHY

World-leading hub of visual culture

Cornell Capa founded ICP in 1974 to honour his brother Robert, an acclaimed war photojournalist killed by a landmine in Vietnam, seeking to share images that capture and change the world. Among its collection are photographs of abolitionist Sojourner Truth, images of lower Manhattan on 9/11 and a pre-moon landing shot taken by NASA in 1966. They also branch out with exhibitions and thematic shows spotlighting topics from street photography to the Spanish Civil War. You can even pair your visit with a workshop on documentary photography or really get into the swing of things with an online class on 'the art of seeing'.

79 Essex Street, New York, NY 10002
Nearest station: Delancey Street–Essex Street
icp.org

72

MOMA

New York's temple to modern art

Midtown isn't often celebrated for its virtues; swarming with offices and chain shops, it's also home to Times Square, which New Yorkers will readily tell you is Dante's ninth circle of hell. And yet, MoMA is still worth braving all these hurdles. The collection features 200,000 works; highlights include a triptych of Monet's *Water Lilies*, Van Gogh's *Starry Night* and Andy Warhol's *Campbell's Soup Cans*. The museum is almost perennially busy, but weekday afternoons tend to be quietest (just don't turn up on a rainy day). Be sure to bring a pair of headphones to enjoy the free Bloomberg Connects app, which guides visitors around the collection. Don't forget to save your ticket, which grants you free admission to the experimental MoMA PS1 in Queens for the following 14 days.

11 W 53rd Street, New York, NY 10019
Nearest station: 5th Avenue/53rd Street
moma.org

73

9/11 MEMORIAL & MUSEUM

Powerful place of remembrance

Every New Yorker who lived through 9/11 has stories to tell, from the day itself when the air was full of smoke and ash, to the following weeks, months and years as the city grappled with its loss. Where the towers once stood, the earth now sinks deep into two square craters lined with bronze, inscribed with the names of the nearly 3,000 people killed that day. Even standing before One World Trade Center, the tallest building in the Western Hemisphere, the waterfalls that pour from each side of the memorial will draw your eyes downwards. Liberty Park, a small elevated green space just by the south pool, is a good spot to take a reflective pause.

180 Greenwich Street, New York, NY 10007
Nearest station: WTC Cortlandt
911memorial.org

74

THE PARK
AVENUE ARMORY

An artsy second act

Built in the late 1800s, the Park Avenue Armory debuted as an arts hub in 2007, with a restoration project still ongoing. At its heart is the massive 55,000 square-foot Drill Hall, an exhibition space that previously held Ann Hamilton's joyful multi-sensory installation *The Event of a Thread*, which saw 42 swings suspended from the 80-foot high, barrel-vaulted ceiling. More recently, trees were hung upside-down over an audience for *Illinoise*, set to Sufjan Stevens' indie music masterpiece and choreographed by Justin Peck. The Recital Series features chamber music and some smaller works and is held in beautifully refurbished spaces like the Board of Officers Room, with stern officer portraits and dark wood details.

643 Park Avenue, New York, NY 10065
Nearest station: 68th Street–Hunter College
armoryonpark.org

75

DAVID ZWIRNER

Contemporary art superstar

In a city where the standard admissions fee to the best art museums hovers around the $30 mark, galleries like David Zwirner offer blissful opportunities to take in outstanding pieces for free. With four galleries in New York – including their striking concrete-and-glass headquarters designed by Annabelle Selldorf on 20th Street – David Zwirner is a heavy hitter in the contemporary art world and represents artists like sculptor Richard Serra, known for his enormous sheets of rusted steel, minimalist Donald Judd and portraitist Alice Neel. Two of the galleries are around the corner from one another in far west Chelsea, so there's plenty to see without much travel.

537 W 20th Street, New York, NY 10011
Nearest station: 23rd Street (C/E)
Other locations: Upper East Side, Tribeca
davidzwirner.com

David Zwirner

76

THE NOGUCHI MUSEUM

Tailor-made space for innovative sculpture

Known for his delicate Akari lights made of trans-lucent paper and wire, Isamu Noguchi was one of the country's most innovative 20th-century sculptors, and the first artist in the US to establish, design and install a museum to display their work. Today, it is a jewel of calm. Occupying the first floor of a repurposed 1920s industrial building, visitors are first treated to the meditative garden filled with trees and shrubs chosen by Noguchi himself, alongside his stone sculptures, including one with water hypnotically running down its surface. The space upstairs holds a revolving door of multidisciplinary exhibitions, with a museum shop filled with Akari lights, books, design homeware and sculptures.

9–01 33rd Road, Queens, NY 11106
Nearest station: Broadway (N/W)
noguchi.org

77

THE PUBLIC THEATER

Theatre institution for all

Theatre is an essential artery that keeps the city's heart beating, and the selection can be dizzying for the uninitiated – Broadway just scratches the surface. Unsure of where to dive in? Start at The Public, one of the country's first nonprofit theatres. The carefully restored Astor Library is home to five theatres and Joe's Pub, a cabaret-style music venue. Shows have included *HAIR*, *Suffs* and, yes, *Hamilton* (which incidentally started here). Don't miss their signature Shakespeare in the Park, the legendary free summertime programme at Central Park's Delacorte Theater (slated to reopen in 2025). If you're hungry for a post-show snack, Los Tacos No. 1 and Levain Bakery, selling excellent tacos and hefty cookies respectively, are just down the street and stay open late.

425 Lafayette Street, New York, NY 10003
Nearest station: Astor Place
publictheater.org

78

CUBBYHOLE

Beloved queer clubhouse

Cubbyhole has witnessed the rise, fall and resurgence of numerous queer spaces from its charming corner in the West Village, and regulars will tell you it's one of the last lesbian bars left in the city. It's a clubhouse where the old guard will always run into each other, but also somewhere that newbies will find friendly faces and serendipitous encounters. The positivity is matched by the joyful decor: disco balls, brightly coloured lanterns and various curios hang overhead. If you're feeling bold enough to belt out a song, pick one from the jukebox in the back. Word to the wise: Cubbyhole keeps things old school and operates on a cash-only basis.

281 West 12th Street, New York, NY 10014
Nearest station: 14th Street (A/C/E/L)
cubbyholebar.com

79

LEYENDA

Drinking south of the border

Award-winning bartenders Julie Reiner and Ivy Mix are the brains behind this moody cocktail haunt on Boerum Hill's bustling Smith Street. The centrepiece of the decade-old space is a bar decked out with mounted shelves and bottle-lined cabinets. Inspired by Central and Latin America, with a distinct leaning towards mezcal, tequila and rum, their Tia Mia with Jamaican rum, mezcal espadin, dry curaçao, orgeat and lime is best enjoyed in the bar's backyard on a steamy summer evening. Pithy tasting notes – 'crisp & smoky' or 'rejuvenating & earthy' – will help you make a decision, and there's the 25+ page spirit list with explanations for those of us who aren't as well versed in the world of agave.

221 Smith Street, Brooklyn, NY 11201
Nearest station: Bergen Streets (F)
leyendabk.com

80
SUGAR MONK

Serious sipping in a seriously inviting space

Around the corner from the legendary Apollo Theater – where Ella Fitzgerald, Aretha Franklin and Billie Holiday all performed – is Sugar Monk, a very seductive cocktail bar. Settle into one of the green velvet chairs and peruse the lengthy menu, which is helpfully divided into categories like the bright and enlivening 'cocktails of ascension' and headier 'cocktails of contemplation' – or opt for one of the non-alcoholic 'cocktails of temperance'. To really kick things off, sample some of the unique concoctions created with Sugar Monk's yield from their Brooklyn micro-distillery. The drinks can be quite strong, so plan on one before or after dinner – perhaps at Sylvia's Restaurant, a Harlem institution just a few blocks away. On Monday nights, Sugar Monk hosts intimate jazz performances with Prohibition-era cocktails.

2292 Frederick Douglass Boulevard, New York, NY 10027
Nearest station: 125th Street (A/B/C/D)
sugarmonklounge.com

81

FINBACK

Drink your way through the neighbourhood

Brooklyn's Gowanus neighbourhood has had a major glow-up in recent years – large industrial spaces have been transformed into climbing gyms, shuffleboard clubs and, crucially, a smattering of breweries and taprooms. Finback is the best around for a glass of something malty and complex, with a bright and inviting high-top tables at which you might (too) easily find yourself perched for the evening. If you can tear yourself away, devotees of the grain should meander onwards in a hoppy haze towards the stylish backyard at Threes Brewing, then Wild East Brewing for a pale ale and finally over to Strong Rope Brewery for hop-forward brews.

545 President Street, Brooklyn, NY 11215
Nearest station: Union Street
finbackbrewery.com

82

THE LONG ISLAND BAR

Neon-lit cocktails

First opened in 1951, The Long Island Bar & Restaurant was family-run for over 50 years. After a protracted hibernation, it was relaunched in 2013 by restaurateur Joel Tompkins and barman Toby Cecchini (inventor of the Cosmopolitan), who kept some of the cosy retro design intact. The cocktail menu is tight and unchanging. There's no trend-chasing here, just a focus on exceptionally well-executed classics like a Boulevardier and Cognac French 75, plus a spicy Dolores del Rio, made with jalapeño-infused tequila. Imbibe more than one, and you'll definitely need to order the double-stacked L. I. Burger.

110 Atlantic Avenue, Brooklyn, NY 11201
Nearest station: Borough Hall
thelongislandbar.com

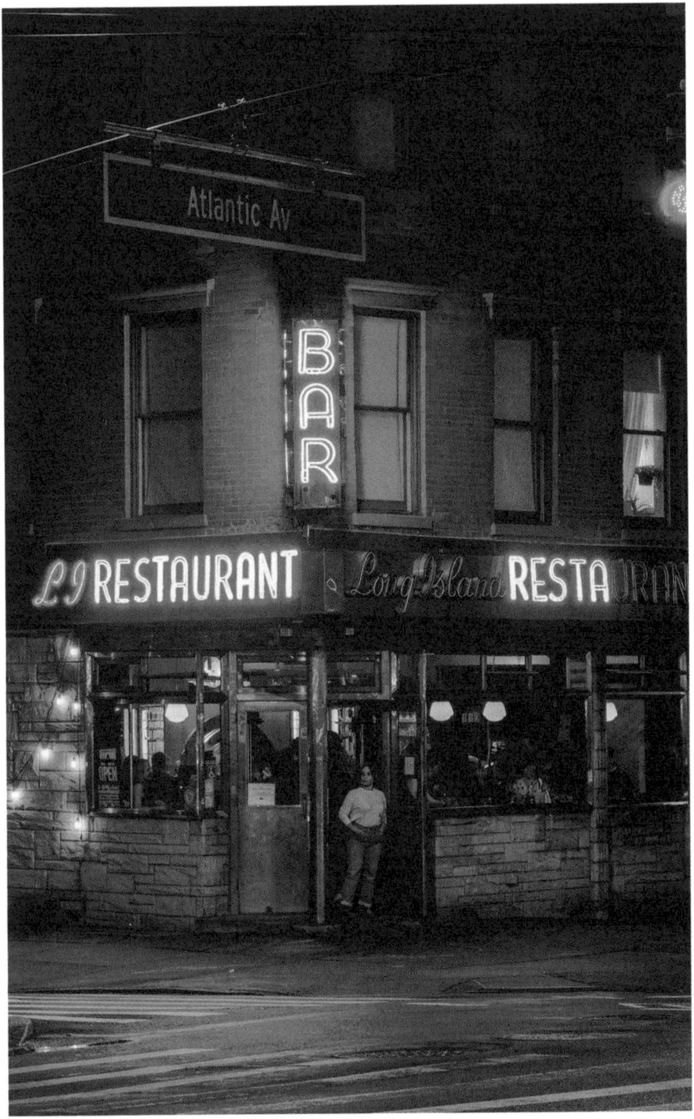
Atlantic Av
BAR
LI RESTAURANT
Long Island RESTA
OPEN

83

DOUBLE CHICKEN PLEASE

Liquid cuisine

Waldorf salad, shroom ceviche and cold pizza are all on the menu at The Coop, the back room at Double Chicken Please. Here's the catch: they come in liquid form. Scoring the top spot on North America's 50 Best Bars list in 2023, Double Chicken Please turns out some of the most innovative drinks in the city. It's a twofer: the Front Room pours Asian-inflected drinks from a series of taps like #5 with whiskey, longan, orange and oolong honey. The food-mimicking libations are further in at The Coop, with dark wooden panelling, cosy banquettes and a bar that doubles as a stage for the mixologists. Drinks are intriguing, require an open mind and are perfect with a koji cucumber snack on the side.

115 Allen Street, New York, NY 10002
Nearest station: Delancey Street–Essex Street
doublechickenplease.com

84

JUNE

Midnight in Paris – in NYC

Henry Rich and his team at The Oberon Group perfected the cosy, intimate Brooklyn vibe at their spots, which are beloved neighborhood gems. But June, their wine bar in Cobble Hill, is their most romantic spot. Featuring soft lighting and a design by hOmE Studios that evokes a vintage Parisian postcard, June is the perfect setting for a seductive date. The extensive list leans towards natural bottles, with two full pages dedicated to skin-contact wines. If you prefer, about ten wines are offered by the glass, and the friendly staff are ready to guide you to a perfect choice. The back patio and yard, which is shaded by a giant tree, is also a dreamy spot for an afternoon drink.

231 Court Street, Brooklyn, NY 11201
Nearest station: Bergen Street (F)
junebk.com

NIGHTLIFE

85

LINCOLN CENTER FOR THE PERFORMING ARTS

Standing ovations aplenty

Home to 20 performance venues for jazz, film, opera, classic music, dance and other performing arts, it's almost challenging to overstate the wonder that is Lincoln Center. Still, it is vital to acknowledge the once-thriving Black and Puerto Rican community that stood here. Among Lincoln Center's strongest offerings include the New York City Ballet and appearances from the American Ballet Theater. While the former is known for its Balanchine aesthetic and more contemporary pieces, the latter often performs more classic, story-based works. Whether a piece is to your taste or not, we defy you to find a bad performance here.

Lincoln Center Plaza, New York, NY 10023
Nearest station: 66th Street–Lincoln Center
lincolncenter.org/home

86

METROGRAPH

Arthouse cinema without the pretence

Striking a delicate balance between film nerdery and downtown cool, this arthouse cinema is as likely to be screening 35mm classics like 1950s French thriller *Rififi* as it is *Batman* and indie films from Southeast Asia. The team drew inspiration from the New York movie theatres of the 1920s, swapping inelegant loungers for velvet-covered chairs fit for the opera. There's a restaurant upstairs and, downstairs, a monochrome bar with a retro-inspired concession stand and the chicest bags of popcorn you've ever seen, plus a curated selection of candy ranging from M&Ms to Swedish Fish and Japanese fruit gummies.

7 Ludlow Street, New York, NY 10002
Nearest station: East Broadway
metrograph.com

87

SMALLS JAZZ CLUB

Jazzy basement in the Village

Some argue you aren't truly a New Yorker until you can stroll down a block and say, 'This bar used to be here', or, 'That shop was once a bodega'. But some icons endure. Smalls, which opened in 1994, is one of them. Breeze down West 10th street and you could easily miss it – the only sign of life above ground is a narrow maroon awning and a line of jazz fans outside. In the underground lair, all eyes are trained on a barely elevated stage complete with piano, drumset and musicians. Even if you're not a jazz aficionado, you should visit to be transported to old New York. The space barely sleeps on the weekend, hosting shows and jam sessions from afternoon until the small hours.

183 W 10th St, New York, NY 10014
Nearest station: Christopher Street–Stonewall
smallslive.com

88

NINE ORCHARD

Rest your head in a vintage bank

It took 12 years to bring this boutique hotel to life on the Lower East Side – corners were not cut. Located in the impeccably restored neo-Renaissance Jarmulowsky Bank from 1912, it's a serene but stylish oasis in a rather busy corner of the city. If you can swing the price tag, reserve one of the supreme-view King rooms, which are located on upper floors – some even feature bathtubs next to the windows so you can soak in the city sky-line (don't worry, there are blinds if you don't want to put on a show). There are plenty of excellent places to eat nearby, like seafood destination Cervo's (no.11) and beloved Chinese restaurant Wu's Wonton King (no.4), both of which are just down Canal Street.

9 Orchard Street, New York, NY 10002
Nearest station: East Broadway
nineorchard.com

89
ACE HOTEL BROOKLYN

Chic living

The rooms at the Downtown Brooklyn outpost of
hip hotel chain Ace are an intensely (dare we say,
too intensely) a Brooklyn vibe: raw concrete, mid-
century furniture and floor-to-ceiling windows. If
that's music to your ears, you may be interested to
know that the turntables, leather trays and even
the laundry bags (helpfully emblazoned with the
word 'LAUNDRY') are all for sale. Ask for a
south-facing room, and ideally one that takes in
the Verrazano Bridge and the Brooklyn skyline,
unless you want a panoramic view of the high-rise
next door. Downstairs, the beautifully lit lobby
is a special treat, with an earthy palette, elegant
wood panelling, large tables for remote work and
a sleek bar which hosts DJ residencies.

252 Schermerhorn St, Brooklyn, NY 11217
Nearest station: Hoyt–Schermerhorn Streets
Other location: Midtown
acehotel.com/brooklyn

90

THE HOXTON, WILLIAMSBURG

Upscale social setting

While the nearby Wythe Hotel (no.91) boasts an intimate ambience, the Williamsburg outpost of The Hoxton is all about shared space. Philly chef Michael Solomonov's cafe-bar-restaurant K'far spans nearly the entire sunken ground floor and is filled with sofas populated during the day by a mix of guests and neighbours. Rooms upstairs come in two sizes – the decidedly tiny 'cosy' and the fractionally roomier 'roomy' – gloriously plush beds are topped with The Hoxton's signature velvet headboards and sleek, subway-tiled bathrooms come with bespoke Dusen Dusen linens. Do what you can to get a table at Laser Wolf, Solomonov's white-hot skewer restaurant upstairs.

97 Wythe Avenue, Brooklyn, NY 11249
Nearest station: Bedford Avenue
thehoxton.com/williamsburg

91

WYTHE HOTEL

The original boutique hotel

North Brooklyn has no shortage of high-end hotels these days, but Wythe was the first. Over a dozen years later, it remains chic and sharply maintained, with a more intimate feel than many of its larger neighbours. Located in a former cooperage that built barrels for the sugar industry, the beds were constructed by a local artisan from reclaimed wood. In fact, all the art is locally made and many of the minibar options have a Brooklyn bent, like the custom whiskey from New York Distilling Co. Tables at the on-site restaurant Le Crocodile are hot property, while Bar Blandeau on the sixth floor is perfect for pairing the sunset with a wine of the same hue.

80 Wythe Avenue, Brooklyn, NY 11249
Nearest station: Nassau Avenue
wythehotel.com

IMAGE CREDITS

An Opinionated Guide to New York
First edition

Published in 2024
by Hoxton Mini Press, London
Copyright © Hoxton Mini Press 2024.
All rights reserved.

Text by Devra Ferst
Editing by Zoë Jellicoe
Design and production
by Richard Mason
Proofreading by Florence Ward
Editorial support by Leona Crawford

With thanks to Matthew Young for
initial series design.

Please note: we recommend checking
the websites listed for each entry
before you visit for the latest
information on price, opening times
and pre-booking requirements.

Thank you to all of the individuals
and institutions who have provided
images and arranged permissions.
While every effort has been made to
trace the present copyright holders
we apologise in advance for any
unintentional omission or error,
and would be pleased to insert the
appropriate acknowledgement in any
subsequent edition.

A CIP catalogue record for this book
is available from the British Library.

ISBN: 978-1-914314-72-8

Printed and bound by OZGraf, Poland

Hoxton Mini Press is an environmen-
tally conscious publisher, committed
to offsetting our carbon footprint.
This book is 100 per cent carbon
compensated, with offset purchased
from Stand For Trees.

Every time you order from our
website, we plant a tree:
www.hoxtonminipress.com

FSC
www.fsc.org

MIX
Paper | Supporting
responsible forestry
FSC® C163799

INDEX